Marvelous
MAINE COONS

STURDY! LARGE! LONG-HAIRED!   INTELLIGENT! FRIENDLY! LOYAL!

ABDO
Publishing Company

Pam Scheunemann

Consulting Editor, Diane Craig, M.A./Reading Specialist

Published by ABDO Publishing Company
8000 West 78th Street, Edina, Minnesota 55439.

Printed in the United States.

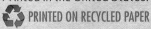 PRINTED ON RECYCLED PAPER

Editor: Liz Salzmann
Content Developer: Nancy Tuminelly
Cover and Interior Design and Production:
   Anders Hanson, Mighty Media
Illustrations: Bob Doucet
Photo Credits: ©Chanan 2009 (pp. 6–7), Shutterstock

Library of Congress Cataloging-in-Publication Data
Scheunemann, Pam, 1955-
 Marvelous maine coons / Pam Scheunemann ; illustrations
by Bob Doucet.
   p. cm. -- (Cat craze)
 ISBN 978-1-60453-723-9
 1. Maine coon cat--Juvenile literature. I. Doucet, Bob. ill. II.
Title.

SF449.M34S34 2010
636.8'3--dc22
                    2009003074

Super SandCastle™ books are created by a team of
professional educators, reading specialists, and content
developers around five essential components—phonemic
awareness, phonics, vocabulary, text comprehension, and
fluency—to assist young readers as they develop reading
skills and strategies and increase their general
knowledge. All books are written, reviewed, and leveled
for guided reading, early reading intervention, and
Accelerated Reader® programs for use in shared, guided,
and independent reading and writing activities to support
a balanced approach to literacy instruction.

CONTENTS

The
MAINE COON

Maine coons are known as gentle
giants. They make good family pets.
They get along well with children and dogs.
Maine coons are one of the larger cat **breeds**.
They are larger than some small dogs!

FACIAL FEATURES

Head

The head of the Maine coon is medium-sized with high cheekbones.

Muzzle

A Maine coon's **muzzle** is somewhat square.

Eyes

The eyes of the Maine coon are large and round. They are set far apart.

Ears

The Maine coon has large ears with tufts of fur. Its ears are high on its head.

BODY BASICS

Size

Adult Maine coons weigh about 8 to 18 pounds (4 to 8 kg).

Build

Maine coons are large and **muscular**.

Tail

Maine coons have long, bushy tails. They are thick at the base and narrow at the tip.

Legs and Feet

Maine coons have sturdy, medium-sized legs. Their paws are round.

COAT & COLOR

Maine Coon Fur

Maine coons are long-haired cats. Their fur is mostly soft and silky. Maine coons should be brushed once a week. This keeps their fur from becoming tangled. Brushing also helps prevent **hairballs**.

CHINCHILLA SILVER

SILVER MACKEREL TABBY

BROWN CLASSIC TABBY WITH WHITE

Maine coons come in many different colors and patterns. The photos on these pages show just a few examples.

The Maine coon has a coat that is good in cold weather. It is thick and keeps water away from the cat's skin. The fur is longer on the legs and stomach. This keeps the Maine coon warm in the snow. The fur is shorter on the back and neck. That way it won't get tangled in plants and bushes.

BLACK SMOKE WITH WHITE

SOLID WHITE

TORTOISESHELL AND WHITE

HEALTH & CARE

Life Span

Maine coons live for
13 years or longer.

Health Concerns

Maine coons are generally
healthy. Some Maine coons
get feline hypertrophic
cardiomyopathy. This is
a type of heart **disease**.
It often just causes a
small **heart murmur**.
But sometimes it results
in heart failure.

VET'S CHECKLIST

- Have your Maine coon spayed or neutered. This will prevent unwanted kittens.

- Visit a vet for regular checkups.

- Brush your Maine coon's fur every week to prevent tangles and hairballs.

- Ask your vet which foods are right for your Maine coon.

- Brush your Maine coon's teeth every day.

- Ask your vet about shots that may benefit your cat.

ATTITUDE & BEHAVIOR

Personality

Maine coons are gentle. They like to be in the same room with their owners. But they don't usually want to be on your lap. Maine coons don't meow very often. They make a chirping sound that is unique to their **breed**.

Activity Level

Maine coons are relaxed. Some of them like the water and will go swimming!

All About Me

Hi! My name is Mack. I'm a Maine coon. I just wanted to let you know a few things about me. I made some lists below of things I like and dislike. Check them out!

Things I Like

- Climbing tall objects or furniture
- Being around my family
- Lying on the couch
- Eating at the same time as others
- Playing with toys
- Exploring my surroundings
- Catching mice
- Playing with water

Things I Dislike

- Being bored
- Being kept in small spaces
- Strangers
- Not being included in my family's activities
- Sitting on someone's lap

LITTERS & KITTENS

Litter Size

Female Maine coons usually give birth to five to seven kittens.

Diet

Newborn kittens drink their mother's milk. They can begin to eat kitten food when they are about eight weeks old. Kitten food is different from cat food. It has extra **protein**, fat, and **vitamins** that help kittens grow.

Growth

Maine coon kittens should stay with their mothers for at least 12 weeks. Maine coon kittens grow more slowly than other cat **breeds**. They are not fully grown until they are three to four years old.

13

BUYING A MAINE COON

Choosing a Breeder

It's best to buy a kitten from a **breeder**, not a pet store. When you visit a cat breeder, ask to see the mother and father of the kittens. Make sure the parents are healthy, friendly, and well behaved.

Picking a Kitten

Choose a kitten that isn't too active or too shy. If you sit down, some of the kittens may come over to you. One of them might be the right one for you!

Is It the Right Cat for You?

Buying a cat is a big decision. You'll want to make sure your new pet suits your lifestyle.

Get out a piece of paper. Draw a line down the middle.

Read the statements listed here. Each time you agree with a statement from the left column, make a mark on the left side of your paper. When you agree with a statement from the right column, make a mark on the right side of your paper.

I don't need to cuddle with my cat.	☐	☐	I want a lap cat.
I enjoy brushing my cat.	☐	☐	I don't like brushing my cat.
I want a cat that is good at catching mice.	☐	☐	I don't care if my cat can catch mice.
I like big cats.	☐	☐	I like small cats.
I don't mind if my cat sheds a lot.	☐	☐	I like a cat that doesn't shed.

If you made more marks on the left side than on the right side, a Maine coon may be the right cat for you! If you made more marks on the right side of your paper, you might want to consider another breed.

Some Things You'll Need

Cats go to the bathroom in a **litter box**. It should be kept in a quiet place. Most cats learn to use their litter box all by themselves. You just have to show them where it is! The dirty **litter** should be scooped out every day. The litter should be changed completely every week.

Your cat's **food and water dishes** should be wide and shallow. This helps your cat keep its whiskers clean. The dishes should be in a different area than the litter box. Cats do not like to eat and go to the bathroom in the same area.

Cats love to scratch! **Scratching posts** help keep cats from scratching the furniture. The scratching post should be taller than your cat. It should have a wide, heavy base so it won't tip over.

Cats are natural predators. Without small animals to hunt, cats may become bored and unhappy. **Cat toys** can satisfy your cat's need to chase and capture. They will help keep your cat entertained and happy.

Cats should not play with balls of yarn or string. If they accidentally eat the yarn, they could get sick.

Cat claws should be trimmed regularly with special cat claw **clippers**. Regular nail clippers will also work. Some people choose to have their cat's claws removed by a vet. But most vets and animal rights groups think declawing is cruel.

You should comb your cat regularly with a **cat hair comb**. This will help keep its coat healthy and clean.

A **cat bed** will give your cat a safe, comfortable place to sleep.

LIVING WITH A MAINE COON

Being a Good Companion

Although Maine coons are large, they are also gentle. They usually get along with other cats and dogs. A Maine coon may be closer to one person in the family. But it will be friendly to other family members too.

Inside or Outside?

Maine coons have heavy coats to keep them warm in cold weather. Maine coons enjoy being able to go outside to play and hunt. However, most vets and **breeders** say that it is best for cats to be kept inside. That way the cats are safe from predators and cars.

Feeding Your Maine Coon

Maine coons may be fed regular cat food. Your vet can help you choose the best food for your cat.

Cleaning the Litter Box

Like all cats, Maine coons like to be clean. They don't like smelly or dirty litter boxes. If the litter box is dirty, they may go to the bathroom somewhere else. Ask your vet for advice if your cat isn't using its box.

DANGER: POISONOUS FOODS

Some people like to feed their cats table scraps. Here are some human foods that can make cats sick.

TOMATOES

POTATOES

ONIONS

GARLIC

CHOCOLATE

GRAPES

THE MYSTERIOUS MAINE COON

No one is really sure how this **breed** began. Some people think shorthair cats in Maine mixed with longhair cats from overseas. Cats were often kept on ships to catch mice and rats. When ships docked in Maine, some cats would go on shore! They may have had kittens with the local cats and created a new breed!

Another mystery is why they are called Maine coons. It could be because their bushy tails make them look a bit like raccoons. Some people think they were named after Captain Charles Coon.

FIND THE
MAINE COON

A

B

C

D

THE MAINE COON QUIZ

1. Maine coons are small cats. **True or false?**

2. Maine coons have round paws. **True or false?**

3. Maine coons have longer fur on their necks. **True or false?**

4. Maine coons make a chirping sound. **True or false?**

5. Some Maine coons like to swim. **True or false?**

6. A Maine coon should stay with its mom until it is 12 weeks old. **True or false?**

GLOSSARY

breed – a group of animals or plants with common ancestors. A *breeder* is someone whose job is to breed certain animals or plants.

disease – a sickness.

hairball – fur that has formed a clump in a cat's stomach. It can cause the cat to throw up.

heart murmur – when the heart doesn't beat normally.

muscular – having a lot of strong muscles.

muzzle – an animal's nose and jaws.

protein – a substance found in all plant and animal cells.

vitamin – a substance needed for good health, found naturally in plants and meats.

About SUPER SANDCASTLE™

Bigger Books for Emerging Readers
Grades K–4

Created for library, classroom, and at-home use, Super SandCastle™ books support and engage young readers as they develop and build literacy skills and will increase their general knowledge about the world around them. Super SandCastle™ books are part of SandCastle™, the leading preK–3 imprint for emerging and beginning readers. Super SandCastle™ features a larger trim size for more reading fun.

Let Us Know

Super SandCastle™ would like to hear your stories about reading this book. What was your favorite page? Was there something hard that you needed help with? Share the ups and downs of learning to read. We want to hear from you! Send us an e-mail.

sandcastle@abdopublishing.com

Contact us for a complete list of SandCastle™, Super SandCastle™, and other nonfiction and fiction titles from ABDO Publishing Company.

www.abdopublishing.com • 8000 West 78th Street Edina, MN 55439 • 800-800-1312 • 952-831-1632 fax